Shades of Sadness...

that keep us on the path to clarity, wisdom, and contentment

Lawrence j.w. Cooper

1

I would be honored if you wanted to copy any part of this book and pass on the message within. I would appreciate recognition and a gentle nudge towards the purchase of this book on Amazon or by contacting me at:

lawrencejwcooper@gmail.com

My Three Ravens Logo

The Raven is a clan ancestor and major character in the beliefs of the Northwest Coast First Nations on whose ancestral lands I live, work, play, and have my being. It is the land I love. My logo features three ravens. The first is the Raven of Compassion who is instructing the Ravens of Knowledge and Wisdom. These three voices together are the voices of transformation. Like the Raven, my desire is to help people realize the basic truth that the sorrows of life can be used to make us stronger and wiser.

Ode to the Raven

Fly, my dear friend, fly.

You who demonstrates the beauty of black,
you who has absorbed all the divine energy
that had been hidden from the eyes of man,
please share the light of *KNOWING* with me
so I can consciously create a path to purpose.
Oh please let me fly with you to your place on high.
Let me reveal to my world a space above the clouds,
beyond the opaque thoughts that block the truth,
beyond the fragile fears that keep us from thriving,
so together we can spread the truth to those lost
in the darkness of their own minds.

Fly, my dear friend, fly.
Soar above the dying Earth.
Soar above the lost humanity
who see only what they want to see
oblivious to the light of truth that brings life.

This book is dedicated to my dear friend, Dan, who gave me a book called 'The Dictionary of Obscure Sorrows' by John Koenig[1]. Many of the comments before each poem are a paraphrase or a direct quote from this book.

---

[1] Koenig, John; *The Dictionary of Obscure Sorrows*. Simon and Schuster; New York. 2021

'It is a calming thing to learn there is a word for something you've felt all your life but didn't know it was shared by anyone else. It is even oddly empowering - to be reminded that you are not alone, you're not crazy, you're just an ordinary human being trying to make your own way through a bizarre set of circumstances.'

(Koenig p. x-xii)

Shades of Sadness

I want to write a poem today,
not because I feel inspired
but just to write a poem today,
to reach into my soul
and find something to write about
to break the monotony of perpetual motion,
to break the monotony of my mind
struggling to be what it is not and cannot be.

I want to write a poem today,
to say the world is beautiful,
but dark clouds have smothered my vision,
and my mind cannot perceive any beauty there.
So I go deeper into my soul
in hopes of finding beauty in just being,
but the world of my mind is resisting
the rising of the morning sun.

So I guess I will just have to live with this day,
and write about the sorrow,
and contemplate the beauty of this foreign world,
the beauty of the other side,
the beauty of my perpetual struggle with sadness.

And so I choose to absorb the substance of all that is
            the good and the bad,
            the beautiful and the ugly,
            the bitter and the sweet,
            the joy and the grief,
until my brain knows it's okay
to see, to smell, to taste, to sense
all the flavors of all the shades of sadness.

The Sadness Begins

Lies so sweet settle like snowflakes,
covering passion with a blanket of white,
and the cold season begins again,
without warmth, without vitality.
It is a time to seek a warm fire,
and snuggle into the folds of a hot body,
and enter into the world of sweet dreams.

But sometimes they are just dreams.
Sometimes there is no warm fire.
Sometimes there is no hot body,
and you find you are alone,
buried under the cold blanket of white,
and you feel the loneliness,
and you face the cold reality,
that in this life you are always truly alone,
alone with your own thoughts,
alone with your own feelings,
feelings that can never be shared
with someone who says they love you,
because they are beyond the grasp of words.

And then, inevitably, you have to learn
to wrap yourself up with yourself,
dance to the beat of your own heart,
and seek the goodness of your own soul.
Then at night you can collapse
into your own snug bed,
and say it is okay to be alone,
because you can sleep with yourself,
and know there is a spirit of love
that is always there in the bed beside you.

Shades off Sadness
from the Past

My Life Story

*The feeling that your life story does not make sense
anymore.* (Koenig p. ix)

This story I have created, a guide
to help me make sense of my life,
does not make sense anymore.
Somewhere, somehow
I have lost control of the plot.
It has taken on a life of its own.
Strange passages have filled the pages,
with a theme I just don't understand,
telling me I am a victim of my own body,
> of my own mind.
Everything I do is beyond my control.

Stanzas have been added by a ghost writer.
who has changed the genre to paranormal.
Everything now seems supernatural.
These words, sentences, and paragraphs
describe an unknow person,
a shifting shadow of who I was.

I seek a touch of normal.
I go back every day and reread past chapters
that I had just skimmed over
in my rush to get to a happy ending.
I try to recapture the wasted moments
that were deleted because I assumed
> they were just fillers.
In one chapter I watch my son run up mountains.
In another I teach my daughter how to ride a bike.

In another I lay on my bed beside my wife
chatting and laughing at the close of the day
about the strange things our four children have done.

These memories help me realize that all is not lost.
These celebrations are still a part of the main plot
where the hero evolves into a powerful person.
My story is not fiction but an essential truth.
> I am the hero of my own story.
> I am the creator of my own life.
> I am who I am. I am my own truth.

As I blend these memories into the present
> I begin to weave in a new plot
> with a clear theme
where I no longer waste precious moments
> regretting the past
but create a string of new smiles and laughs.
I write a new chapter filled with fillers
that contribute to a new meaning to life.

Then someday those precious ones who follows me
may be inspired by my *Shades of Sadness*,
> understand my theme,
and decide to create a sad story of their own
filled with a thousand fillers of the sweet reality
where they are loved from the beginning to the end.

The World I Left Behind

'The eerie feeling of seeing a place abandoned that was once full of people'.

(Koenig p. ix)

My hometown, North Battleford,
a little town on the prairies
where the sadness started.
Folks from the farms
came to town on rainy Saturdays
to shop and take care of business.
The downtown is empty of people now,
the old familiar stores
demolished or shuttered.

So many memories...
Ernie's barber shop
where I had my proud Elvis duck-tails,
        with a cute kiss curl,
cruelly clipped each month....
the Baccus Bothers Pool Room
where the boys and I played
eight ball, snooker, and billiards.
I was pretty good at billiards
        on the big tables...
Tom's diner
where my friends and I
sipped our root beer floats
and dropped nickels into the little jute box
waiting eagerly at the end of each table,
my favorite *Don't be Cruel*
        to a heart that's true
played over and over again
until I ran out of nickels.

St Thomas College, my old high school,
they ran out of priests to teach,
is now a government office building,
the chapel where I got married,
now an art gallery...
across town the Convent of the Child Jesus
lies in ruins deprived of young female voices,
the add-on gym now a Pentecostal church....
across town the public collegiate gone
where I had my first dance
with the first girl I ever loved
who invited me to come and sway
on Sadie Hawkins day.

An eerie feeling floods my soul.
Memories lie abandoned on the empty streets.
Faces fade into the evening twilight.
I feel the heaviness of having never left,
the sensation of having left part of me behind.

My Childhood Home

The sadness I feel when I visit places I have once lived.

I visit my old hometown.
I drive past my old home,
still there after all these years.
I can't look at it.
I want to,
but I don't want to.
I try not to.
I tell myself to look away
but I look anyway.
I can't help myself,
even though there is nothing
I want to see there,
nothing I want to remember.

Memories hurt.
When I see... I think.
When I think... I feel.
I don't like to feel.
I don't like to relive the sadness.

I close my eyes and count to five
and let my car drift slowly past.
When I feel safe again, I open my eyes.
As I turn left at the next corner
I risk a glimpse in the rear-view mirror.
I take a deep breath,
        accelerate,
and race away from the past
and back into the present.

Home

The sadness of never having a place to call home.

My home?
I have no idea where it is...
...or was...

Almost every childhood home I lived in
was torn down or burned after we left,
practice for volunteer fire fighters.

My homes,
the ones I built with the sweat of my brow,
were never really mine.
They belonged to my wife and children.
        I just lived there.

I have had no sense of belonging,
        no sense of direction.
I was pulled everywhere and nowhere
by the spirit of restlessness that dwelt in me,
and the people who controlled my thoughts,
making it impossible to rationally navigate
        through the chaos,
making it impossible to have a home
to anchor me in one place at any point in time,
so that I could safely live in the present.

Now that I have passed the age of reason
and entered the age of visions and dreams,
I have finally discovered that a home
        was never meant to be.

I am just a wanderer passing through
on my way to I know not where.
But I have learned to sit back
and enjoy the sunshine on my face,
the wet rain that dampens the fire.
   I grow my precious flowers
   and walk my sacred paths
where joy lives and peace abides.

Sharing Secrets

The sadness of giving up talking about an experience
because people are unable to relate to it.

(Koenig p.15)

I have secrets
that I just pretend to share
disguising my feelings with clever words.
Counsellors have listened
because I paid them.
I have partially confessed to special friends
who share a common experience
because I know they will smile at me
and perhaps even laugh with me,
but they do not want to cry with me.

I am careful with my secrets.
I feel shame when I relate them.
I avoid the judgement of people
who say they love me
        because I fear
they do not love me unconditionally.

Even worse
I fear their response may be casual.
They haven't really listened.
They don't really care.
Then my greatest fear washes over me.
        I am always be alone.

How can they possibly understand
unless they have walked a mile in my moccasins,
unless they have cried with me

when we get to the sad part,
unless they have paused long enough
to see the sunshine and the rain
that follows the season of sadness.

These experiences are mine, mine alone.
I lived through them and in them.
I have walked in light and in darkness.
I have tasted of the forbidden fruit.
I now understand that good and evil
are two halves of the same apple
that has fallen from the Tree of Life.
I have bitten into the bitter-sweetness.
The knowledge of good and evil is now inside me.

And yet, I still long to tell my story
to everyone I intimately meet
in the hopes that they too can laugh and cry
      at the intensity,
      at the innocence,
      at the broken dreams
      at the nightmares
in which we all share our humanity.

Past Lovers

The sadness of remembering the darkest shades of sadness from the past... past lovers.

Poems, my therapy.
Am I holding back, hiding from the therapist,
avoiding the truth from the past again?
Maybe, but how can I possibly
put my feelings into words,
and even if I could,
would I want to share them with anyone?
Even with my therapist?
Even with the anonymous writer of these poems?

So I keep things mystical, poetic,
disguised in images
that jumble all my lovers,
      my exes,
          into symbols,
      just metaphors
to describe how they made me feel...
      agitated,
      starved,
      strangled.
Why can't I ever get what I want?
Why can't my lovers give me peace?

If I could just focus on the moment
without knowing
where the next high is coming from,
then maybe the poet
could translate my feelings into words.
Maybe the therapist

could shed light on why
I feel the sadness I feel.

Perhaps if I compact all my emotions
          into just one word,
one word that can say it all,
newspeak come alive among the dead,
a language that could hide all my emotions...

          HOLLOWNESS,
something that can never be fixed,
          a hole that is permanent.
Perhaps it is not too late to grow myself around it
like the old trees on my favorite forest path
that extend their roots through huge rocks.
Perhaps if I could curl my mind
around the rock of rocks,
the mother of my children,
I could finally hide her from my consciousness.

          HOLLOWNESS,
It says all these things I know and don't know,
all the things I don't want to know.
But hollow does not really describe this feeling.
It is much more complex than just one word.
It is much more complex than just one feeling.
These feelings are filled with so much rubble
          that they are impenetrable,
               unbreakable,
          rocks protecting rocks
     protecting the mother of all rocks.

Perhaps if I try hard enough I can cover them up
          with an avalanche of words

and create a sanctuary of peace
away from my conscious mind.
Perhaps I can add a few more metaphors
to distract me from this feeling
         of never feeling loved
         just for who I am.

Perhaps I should write a poem that defines
this feeling that is so much more complex than
         HOLLOWNESS...
but then I could never let anyone read it.
I could never read it to my prying therapist.
I could never share it with the blind poet
because it might strip him of his ability
to disguise his feelings with words.

It is June 29th again,
the golden anniversary that could have been.
Perhaps I can dare to remember
that there were 33 good years,
some of them great years,
good memories buried beneath the rubble.
Perhaps I can dare to remember
         making love was real,
         being in love was real.
Perhaps I can finally acknowledge
that the memories are now a part of me,
         a good part of me.
Perhaps it's okay to remember
that the love I received was real
that the love I gave was real.
Perhaps it's okay to remember that I have loved.
Perhaps it's okay to let myself be sad today.

The Sound of Silence

'The lulling sensation of driving late at night-floating
through the void in an otherworldly hum.'

(Koenig p 25)

I used to like driving on a warm summer night
with the sunroof open and the windows down.
I used to enjoy the cool wind in my hair
blowing away the hot thoughts of a summer day.

I drifted down quiet city streets with my bulldog,
her head stuck defiantly out the passenger window.
We enjoyed the neon colors that pierced the dark
penetrating the shades of sadness that dwelt there.

I enjoyed the sounds of sad music on the car stereo...
Simon and Garfunkel... *The Boxer... I Am a Rock.*
It reminded me that sadness can be captured in song
played over and over again until the pain disappears.

Eventually all that was left was a peaceful hum.
I sang along to the Sound of Silence,
  'Hello darkness my old friend
  I've come to talk with you again',
until the only thing I felt was the hum of words
that drained the swamp of sad feelings
  from my sullied mind.

Shades of Sadness Created by my Own Mind

What I Really Want

Feeling torn between the life you want and the life you have.

(Koenig p.17)

I want it all.
I want to experience everything my body can feel
        while this body can still feel.
I want to explore the full range of possibilities
        while my brain can still imagine.
I want to see what has never been seen
and hold those images in my mind forever.
I want to visit every country that is on the map
and all the ones who have disappeared
erased by the fickleness of time.
I want to sail the seven seas
and get lost in the vast expanse of place and time.
I want to dance with the chaos
until we sway together in harmony.
I want to barge into the place where dreams are kept
and demand they bow to my wishes.
I want my books to be read by a million people,
        hear the harsh criticism of those
            who will never see what I see
                and feel what I feel
                    and laugh.

But is that what I really want?
Or do I just want to enjoy what I already have?
I love watching the sun rise above Denman Island,
and view life's image reflected off the Salish Sea.
I love to sift the dirt with my bare hands
and mindfully prepare my gardens for new life.

I love to sit on Qualicum Bay Beach
and look out across the wide expanse of sea
to the white-capped mountains beyond.
I love to walk my favorite forest paths
and stop to rest my arms around my favorite giants
and thank them for sharing their forest with me.
I love to seek out the young fry
hiding in the roots and rocks of the creek beds
and smile at their courage to try to beat the odds
and make it into the wide-open seas.

My dreams?
I will still dream because that is who I am.
My books? I will still write
because that is what I do.
But I will let be what will be
        and live,
        just live,
and savour every flavor of it.

I Need

The sadness of realizing there is a place in your psyche that can never be filled.

(Koenig p. 30)

I need more food
enough for the day after tomorrow,
more money
to buy more things I do not need,
more years to live
so I can go on believing I will never die,
more praise
so my ego can be proud of itself,
more sales of my books
to prove I am a great poet,
more attention
to prove I have important things to say,
more affection
to be reassured that I am still lovable,
more sex
to prove I am still a man,
more hours of sunshine
to eliminate the darkness of a rainy day,
more joy
to brighten these perpetual shades of sadness.

So sad because I do not see
    I already have
everything I will ever need.

Memories

The awareness that this moment too will become just a memory.

(Koenig p.9)

I can see it now in this moment of bliss,
living with my dearest in our own piece of paradise.
I can feel it now, the joy, this sense of peace,
but I am afraid it cannot last forever.

Memories,
times when I thought it would last,
have betrayed me,
or perhaps I have betrayed them.
I have made decisions that I later regretted.

I believed I was invincible,
that I could control all the possibilities,
that I could force the bliss to last forever.
Those moments are now gone,
replaced by insufficient memories.

Will this moment, too,
disappear into the forever?
Will circumstances dictate
that I may have to start over once again, alone,
too old to let go of now and embrace tomorrow?

Deja Vu, just a repetitive perspective
to confuse a weary mind with sadness
so I can't see the future just like the present,
so I have to re-memorize the past
and make it live again.

The Power to Create a New Now

But I have learned to believe in the power of myself,
and the future seems to be not so bad.
If the present becomes just a memory,
if my dearest becomes just a sweet remembrance,
perhaps I can again rediscover that the now
holds one more unfulfilled desire,
that I still have the power to manifest
one more dream into reality.

Then perhaps the things I hold
will be even more precious,
no longer tangled up in fear.
Perhaps I will have the power
when the time comes
to move on and see how possibilities unfurl,
ride one more wave to the eternal truth
that I can sail the eternal seas within my own soul.
Perhaps I will choose to be vulnerable
                until I will finally know
 how life itself is the only thing that really matters.

The Main Character

The sadness of knowing that each person is the main character of their own story and we are just an extra in the background.

I pass by people everyday,
random bodies in random packages of flesh,
but each is living a life as complex as mine,
each has a heart that longs to tell their own story
to anyone who will listen.

I sip my morning cup of coffee at Tim Hortens
on Blanchard in Victoria
just down the street from Pandora
where the homeless shelter in crude abodes.
I study the people I may see only once.
Some just stop on their way to work,
but I cannot help but notice that others
have come out from under their crude cold tents
with just enough change for a hot drink
        in a warm place.
My heart aches for them and demands I say hello.
I stop awhile to recognize their existence,
add a breakfast sandwich to the conversation,
perhaps leave a twenty on the table
and tell them it's for their next meal.
There is immense value in every life.
There is never a reason to be rude
to anyone who may be experiencing hardship.
I have to continuously remind myself
to treat others like I would like to be treated,
to add a positive sentence to their complex life story
that lies tangled behind each struggling faces.

Being a Part of Intimate Stories

And then I remember to stay totally aware
of the feelings and thoughts of those closest to me
        my friends and family,
            especially my life partner,
to help build them up and support them
and never say or do anything to tear them down,
but to stay just far enough away
to let them write their own story
and be eternally grateful
that they chose to share it with me.

My Pledge

I will be curious about people
on the edge of existence.
I will ask about their hopes and dreams,
but I will keep it light
until I know them better
and they know me better
and trust me to be real.
I will try to laugh with them and not at them.
I will use my empathy skills to feel what they feel.
I will remind myself that a complex life-story
 lies behind each face who ventures into my world.

Angry Voices

'The imaginary committee of elders who keep a running log of all your mistakes.'

(Koenig p. 47)

Voices,
so many voices,
loud angry voices,
a whisper emerging through the fog.
I apologize, my mind filled with shame and remorse.

Voices,
always voices.
I strain to hear the words
of amplified anger accusing me
of trying to have powers I should never have.

Voices,
harsh voices.
I need to challenge them
and send them back to that sad place
that corner of darkness from which they came.

Happy Voices

And then I hear the sound of laughter and love again.
It floods my tired soul with the energy of the infinite.
It urges me to open up my heart and feel the passion
and boldly seek the joy of each and every moment.
I am guided by a force greater than the voices,
beyond hearing and feeling, beyond all my senses.

It tells me that it is okay to keep seeking for meaning
that will allow me grow into the person I want to be,
to believe I can be a loving powerful human being
to believe that my voice can bring compassion
to a world lost in the kind of sorrow
that leads to anger.

Talking to Myself

The sadness of engaging in a pointless hypothetical
conversation with yourself that you compulsively play
out in your head.

I play out my sadness by talking to myself.
I review the problem over and over in my head.
I predict responses and practice my comebacks,
       until I say all the right things,
       until I can win the argument.

But do I?
How would I feel if I got what I think I wanted?
Have I considered how the ones I love would feel
if they had to give in to my thoughts and desires?

So I talk to myself again.
I ask my body how it would feel
if I got what I think I want.
I ask my mind if it has considered all the possibilities
before it has come to its conclusions.
I ask my heart if I have shown love
       for others and for myself.
I ask my soul if I am being true to the me in me
       and the you in you.

We hash it out again.
My aging body says what it can do, what it can't do.
My heart asks if the decision shows compassion.
My soul asks if this is for the greater good.
We argue with each other until we come to the point
where we all agree and the decision is unanimous.
We pat each other on the back. We laugh til we cry.

The Other Me

The sadness of realizing you have blown it again, that you are still human with human feelings that sometimes gets in the way of being the mature lover you want to be.

Sometimes the days are short
and the nights are too long.
A deep darkness seeps into my soul.
A chill wind drives out any warmth
from thoughts of love.
My troubled mind is lost and angry.
My heart is on the verge of tears.

On these days my sense of helplessness
spreads its ugly influence on you,
my dearest, the one I am supposed to love.
Unkind thoughts grow into unkind words.
'I'm sorry' is so damn hard to say,
and I walk away into my own dark world.

During these gray days my madness
eventually collapses in upon itself,
and my heart urges my mind to love again.
I spread a pillow of imaginary roses
for you to rest your weary mind,
and my lips finally find the courage
to desperately say, 'I love you.'

There You Are Again

And there you are again.
You reach out with a warm touch
and I collapse into your snug embrace.
Your kiss brings life back into my tired body.
All the captive words I want to say
escape the prison in my mind,
and I remember all the reasons I love you.

Don't Touch Me

'Compulsively running away from works of art that you find frustratingly nauseatingly good… because it resonates at precisely the right frequency to rattle you to your core which makes it mildly uncomfortable to be yourself.'

(Koenig p. 71)

Some things touch me
where I do not like to be touched,
an invasion of my inner sanctuary
where I keep my deepest feelings.

Like the play *Breaking the Code*,
Alan Turing chemically castrated,
just because he experienced pleasure
by meeting other men in a place
where others would never go,
      a 'thank you'
for saving thousands of lives
with his brilliant mind.
I knew that part of him
was just like that part of me
hiding my feelings behind closed doors
that should never be opened
by anyone who does not truly love me,
by anyone who has ignored
all the good I have done
as a loving husband and father,
as a counsellor for those who suffer.

I cried when I saw the movie *Old Yeller*,
a loving dog shot after contracting rabies
defending his beloved master and friend

from the fangs of a rabid wolf.
It reminds me of my Lassie
who stayed by my side
from age eight to eighteen
as I struggled with my convoluted youth,
with feelings that I had never been loved.
I watched her die on a cold winter night.
I could not cry.

Like the sculpture of the Pieta,
 a mother holding her innocent son
who had been crucified
for telling the world
they needed to love each other.
It reminds me of my mother
who held two dying children in her arms.
She was afraid to hold me
because she thought I too might die
because I too had been conceived in sin.

Sometimes when I read my own poems,
I cry when I see the words
that describe the pain I used to feel,
the curse of my mental issues,
because I was born unwanted
by a single mother with eight children.
All these things are in the distant past
but I still can't help but remember
whenever something touches me
where I do not want to be touched.

It's Time to Cry

As I sit here at my keyboard recalling these things,
I finally cry for the women who tried to love me,
for the mother who did her best to care for me,
and for the dog who adored me till her dying breath.

Brutality

The sadness of realizing that you have spent your whole lie being cruel to the most important person in your life... yourself.

A brutality disguised by disillusioned honesty,
sheltering shame, blame, and unbridled loathing,
preventing a perchance love lesson to be learned
because it lay untouched within the fire
        that consumed me.

This brutality came without compassion,
reserved by me, just for me,
to punish myself for not being perfect,
to hate myself because of the sadness
        of not feeling loved.

So I went gentle into the night
with the only light my core of strength,
that little brave boy in ME
        the ME unseen.

The last few years have been more kind.
I see now that the ME deserved more love,
like the empathy I had bestowed
        on those I had served.

I have become gentler with myself
I have found peace from within
that gentle spirit I had previously shared
        only with others.

The Dancer

The sadness of racializing that you are always truly alone with your own thoughts and feelings and then realizing it's okay to be alone.

The walls close in,
pulsating in rhythm
to the throbbing heart
of the dancer.
The lights flicker and fade,
while the singer repeats the ugly refrain.

All gyrations cease,
giving way to the dark.
The music slows,
the rhythm becoming hypnotic,
trance like.
The dancer, holding tight to chaos,
seeks a rhythm from within,
and dances the dance of time,
alone.

An Aria of Love

The ME I was then and the ME I am now
have come together in perfect harmony,
the pure voice of the child tenor,
the powerful bass of the mature adult,
sing the song of love and life,
hard without brutality, soft without shame.

Shades of Sadness in Nature

Black Clouds

The sadness and peace that goes with being inside during a thunderstorm.

(Koenig pg. 5)

The black clouds roll in
off the dry prairie horizon.
Lightning flashes break through the darkness.
Thunder roars in contempt
for those who cover the land with concrete.
Waves of water pound against the roof.
The ground saturated
forms rivulets that turn into streams,
a steady flow that washes out the gutters.

The wee lad sits and watches
from a window where the water collects
            and then flows upward.
The boy waits till he feels safe
before rushing outside
to launch his boats into the seas
that will carry his dreams to faraway shores.

As another black cloud rolls in,
I release my bent-up emotions,
That touch of fear, the pressure of regret.
I long for the days of youth.
My mind reflects on what it would feel like
            to be young again
and sail my boat into another world
where I can begin to breathe again.

My Castle in the Air

The sadness of wanting to break away from one's career to pursue a simple and pastoral life.

(Koenig pg. 5)

My soul was locked into ninety-hour workweeks.
I strove to impress; I willed myself to succeed.
I wanted to advance my career to show the world
I could be that bright star that shone in the night.
       I sought perfection.

My career kept sucking away my time, my joy,
until my determination destroyed all my dreams.
They became diversions, another burden to bear.
My life was crumbling on the outside.
       I was dying on the inside.

Friendly fantasies fought with hostile realities.
My dreams of stardom became collateral damage.
My overstressed mind created a hypnotic diversion.
It whisked me away from my self-imposed prison
       to a cabin by the sea.

I lived in this duality for thirty-three years until
emotions erupted from the depths of my soul.
The tsunami surge swept away my old life.
Grief shook me until the final collapse.
       It swept away my castle in the air.

       .

A Cabin by the Sea

An early retirement, a well-earned pension
freed me from my prison of doing.
I let Costa Rica restore my mind and body
in my mountain cabin under a live volcano.
        I began to dream again.

My heart began to love again, first life,
than me, then the woman I now love.
We pursued a life with new realites,
a life beyond my wildest dreams,
        a life of endless possibilities.

We now let life drift slowly blissfully by.
As I stare mindfully at the distant shores,
reality is better than I dreamed it could be
with my love and I sharing our home,
        a cedar cabin by the Salish Sea.

A Warm Summer Morning

*'The sadness that happens when you realize that you
are perfectly happy and you consciously try to savor
the feeling which prompts your intellect to identify it,
pick it apart, and put it in context until it's little more
than an aftertaste.'*

(Koenig pg. 5)

A warm summer morning,
I sit on my deck overlooking the Salish Sea,
watching the sky
between Deep Bay and Denman Island
change from dark blues to reds and golds.
With a hot cup of coffee in my hand,
my thoughts slowly, persistently,
drift with the tides.
I savor the moment; I am present in the present.
I am content; I enjoy my state of *being*.

As my self-awareness evolves,
I begin to analyse why I feel this way.
Where I have been? What I have seen?
What has brought me here
to experience this taste of paradise?

The now evaporates
with the heat of my rising thoughts.
The cup of coffee turns cold.
Yesterday and tomorrow
begin to take center stage again,
pushing the present
into the pit of persistent platitudes.
The *why* takes me away from the *what*.

The moment of perfect peace dissolves
taking me back into the world of *doing*.
My jealous mind's eagerness... *to do*
has overruled my soul's desire... *to be*.

A sense of loss envelops me.
My mind examines my emotions
to discover what has destroyed the feeling.
But my soul, ever the perfect player,
assures me that it can all happen again...
   perhaps tomorrow.

Echoes from Baynes Sound

The sadness of a tranquil and rhythmic sounds that put you completely at peace.

The busy sounds on Baynes Sound,
echoes of another time, but the same place,
owned by the creatures who have dwelt here forever
adding their voices to the cacophony of chaos...

> the loonie loon's absurd laugh,
> the *tap-tap-tap* of the northern flickers,
> the *baaaarking* of the sea lions,
> the senseless *chaaaaatter* of the crows.

And man adds to the helter-skelter of chaos
donating to nature's chaotic sounds...
> the *whiiiiine* of the chainsaws,
> the angry *groooowll* of the weed-eaters,
> the heavy *breathththing*
> of the leaf-blowers,
> the monotonous *murrrrrrmurrrrrr*
> of the electric lawnmowers.

But the early morning sounds are quieter.
They *hummmm* in time and tune with the first light.
They usher in a moment of peace...
> the musical lilt of the robin,
> the multitalented loon
> singing her morning mournful song,
> the horned owl giving her final *hoooot*
> before departing in the night.

Not to be outdone
Baynes Sound sends out its soft percussion brooms.
The flat-bottomed oyster-boats dare to swishishishish
in accompaniment to natures softer tones.
They chug slowly along to their waiting flats
to lower their living cargo into the rising tides.
Little filters silently eliminate man's waste.

As I sit her on my deck contemplating life's lie.
every sound contains an element of truth.

Star Gazing

The feeling of sadness by being stuck on earth while looking up to the stars.

(Koenig.p14)

During my loneliest nights
when the whole world looks dark,
I sit in my hot tub looking up at the stars
wondering if tomorrow is worth the effort
it would take to get up in the morning.

I let the feeling of being so small
in such a vast universe
flood my mind
until I realize the only meaning of anything
is the unique invention of my conscious soul.

Then the sparks of light make love to my mind.
They coax it to write another poem of self-love
where the so-small me is just as big
as the biggest star in the sky.
Then I become part of the universe
until I know that I AM the universe
            and the universe is me.

Early Morning Blues

The otherworldly atmosphere before 5 a.m.

(Koenig, p 20)

Summertime is when time stands still.
The sun rises above the Salish Sea at five A.M.
but you can wallow in the shades of blue at 4
and mine the rich lode of gold at 4:45.

But I have been up since 3 a.m.
        unable to sleep.
My age gives way to my speeding mind.
It urgently tries to talk me into spending
four more hours writing another book
that few people will ever read,
       and I wonder:
  'Why the hell am I doing this?'

And then my weary mind gives way to my heart
which admits it is hoping to leave a legacy behind
to remind my grandchildren whom it loves so dearly
that the hours of darkness cannot last forever,
that the sun will always rise at 5 am in June

6 A.M.

Here I am again, waiting, writing.
I pause to welcome the light into my dark world.
My wife greets me with a hug and a kiss.
      The long night ends.
      A new day begins.

Simple Things Make Me Cry

The heartbreaking simplicity of ordinary things.
(Koenig p. 22)

I have climbed the career ladder with some success,
but each rung was gained at such a great cost.
I have lived too long and schemed too hard
to carve out a place in the world of poets.
I have played the game of demanding to be heard
amidst the cacophony of the chaos.
I am an old man now, but it is still not too late
to sit on an old piece of driftwood by the Salish Sea
and watch the endless waves make love to the shore.
Sometimes simple things open the flood gates
        and let me cry.

I watch the mother deer stand on her hind legs,
stretch her tongue to tip the birdfeeder,
and let the sweet grains roll into her mouth.
I realize even deer can think and scheme.
I notice the alpha hummingbird scouting for rivals
chasing them from the sweet waters of the feeder
He reminds me that sharing is better than hoarding.
I watch a pair of raccoons wrestle in the pond I built
knocking over the carefully laid rocks and plants.
I am awed by how animals take time to play.
I see two pairs of ravens frolic in the gale winds
moving in unison through the storm as they fly.
I marvel at how even birds like to dance.
Simple things sometimes break my heart.

It's Not Too Late

These simple things chastise me
knowing how much life I have wasted
pursuing things that will never matter
        when I die.
But I know that it is never too late
to stop scheming and hoarding,
to take time to play and dance,
be a part of all with an open heart,
smile, and take time
        to cry.

Manmade Prisons

The awareness that you are not really at home in the wilderness.

(Koenig p. 27)

I am running away again,
away from asphalt roads and cement sidewalks,
away from people with their concrete view of life
      limited to a 3 by 7 devise,
manmade rules justified by manmade logic,
insisting the world must be the way they say it is.

There is a part of me that longs
to escape this manmade prison
and talk to Mother Sea
while I stroll along her eternal shores
keeping my eyes fixed on the horizon
where truth must surely abide.
Or flee to my favorite forest path
where the only pain I hear
is the crunch of yesterday's leaves.
Perhaps I can stop to stroke the rough bark
of my dear friends, the giants of the forest,
and listen with my heart as they console me,
telling me it's okay to stay in one place forever.
Or perhaps I can eavesdrop on the birds
as they sing about a perfect world
that exists only in their imperfect songs.

And yet I know deep inside
that the Garden of Eden is just a myth
to ignore the harsh reality,
the brutality of killing and eating,
while Mother Nature turns away

indifferent to the violence against the innocent,
abiding by the rules she herself has created
where things must die so other things can live.

All my truths spill from her shattered image.
My dear canine companion becomes
just a domesticated animal
that has been bred to feed on my abilities
        to make the kill.
I realize that I too am just a domesticated animal
        in a perpetual struggle
with other domesticated animals
        striving to garner and hoard
more than my share of the resources
        a better hunter and gatherer,
        to prove that I am alpha
and establish my right to make the rules.

                And then I come face to face
                    with my own reality
                    my own brutality,
                    my own vulnerability,
                knowing there are no real rules
                except the law of kill or be killed.

Being a gentle soul, I seek to survive
the contradiction of my own thoughts.
I disguise my mind in garments of spirituality
and sing hymns to a perfect god
who has created a perfect world
waiting for me on the other side of time
where the lion lies down with the lamb
and the nations of the world
convert their swords to plow shears.

But the waves of the sea,
the rustle of the leaves,
and the melodies of the songbirds,
all sing different songs
played to different tunes
and I realize there is no perfect world.
Heaven is just a fantasy
that people of power have created
to convince the masses
to ignore their own suffering.

My mind realizes there is no perfect world
to flee to where I can take refuge when,
>something,
>someone,
>some thought
challenges my right to exist
my right to be myself.

And then I finally comprehend that there is no need
to accept the stifling bonds of someone else's rules
or to escape the indifference of my own dogmas.
I can bury all my fears and all my sad thoughts
>in my own imperfect world
that I have created thoughtfully, mindfully,
where there is no fear of dying or being eaten.

All just is as it is.
I am who I am,
and today is just another day
to walk my sacred paths
and just enjoy this life I have created
by myself and for myself.

Red and Yellow Blues

'The feelings generated by staring into a fire in the dark during (moments of) depression.'

(Koenig p. 31)

Night has arrived...
>...again...
This is the hard part of the day,
no work and business to distract me
from the knowledge that the dark part
will soon come to consume me...
>...again.

The flames flicker in the fireplace.
Reds dance with yellows.
Passion dances with fear.
I stare deeper and deeper into the flames.
The blues emerge.
They sway to the broken-hearted music.
I slow-step with them
into the desolation of the past
the uncertainties of the future.
I stare past the blues
into the hot coals of the present,
a life lived without purpose and meaning.

A glass of scotch on the rocks,
three fingers,
calms the angst.
My English Bulldog's head
nestles onto my lap.
Her loud snoring grounds the grief
creating a soothing rhythm

that tells me there is life after death.
The intensity of the heat subsides
The blues fade.
The sparks of sorrow begin to settle.
The passion of the reds
slowly disappears with the hours.
The dread of the yellows flickers and dies.

The flame goes out.
Thirty-three years, four children,
                    gone.
All that remains are still-hot embers,
a touch of warmth on a cold winter's night.

The Angry Waves

A momentary trance of emotional clarity.

(Koenig p 77-79)

From this rock on the shores of Long Beach,
I sit alone overlooking the churning sea.
I feel a truth roll in with each angry wave.
My chest shudders as a deep breath arises
from some grave place inside me.

I sense that something is happening,
some surge of emotion
yielding to a cascading watershed of tears,
and yet my mind is not here,
no thoughts, no sorrows, no grief,
just tears without reason, without sad feelings.

I think back to the series of events
that have awakened me
dragging me here kicking, screaming,
to the sad shores of the old Pacific.
I look back at my choices,
my mistakes, my achievements,
at all the things I have won and lost,
the opportunities that came and went,
the breaking of my heart, my loss of self-respect,
the respect of my wife and children,
all the agonizing twists and gut-wrenching surges.

The world keeps shouting at me.
It urges me to make plans for a new future.
But all the things I think I see as truths
are just excuses to keep on living.

My life has become just an experiment.
Like a mad scientist I sit in my lab by the sea
        changing the variables.
I search for the one solution that can pass the test,
One law that can justify my existence.

Quiet Swells

And yet, I can feel sorrow now with gratitude
thankful for life's chances and changes
for its mysteries and blessings.
I see the complexity of things
that will all disappear with my last breath,
that any meaning I am sensing now
exists only in this gush of emotion,
these moments of tears without sadness
that flow through my heart like quiet swells
 gently rolling beyond the angry waves.

I am the Dream

Pain passes with the expansion of my inner me.
I finally realize that I am part
of the immense breath and width of life
that lies beyond the crashing of the angry waves.
I walk out of this dream I have created,
this dream that has recreated me,
that has thrust me into a new reality.
I am in not just in the dream, I am the dream.

A Serene Truth

I cannot stay in this space too long, it is too intense.
My mind folds in on itself leaving a new reality
that life must be lived just to be lived.
This solitary moment must stand on its own
as proof of my sanity, a proof of my existence.

I climb back into my car.
I go back to the business of thinking and living.
But I plan to come back to this rock tomorrow
to see if serene truth still rests here,
or will it have disappeared with the next angry wave.

Tofino

The sadness of watching a time in a special place at a
special time of perfect connection with the one we love
suffer a letdown with another needless argument once
we are back in our daily routines.

Entranced by the full power of the ocean
I stare for hours watching the waves
crash upon the shore, mesmerized,
transported beyond all the cares of my world.
My love strolls the endless beach by my side.
We hold each other's hearts in our hands.
As the cares of this world wane
we see past the dark side of the waves
and step into the light reflected from the crests.

We let the hours slow from their mad pace
to a lifetime of timelessness
where thoughts give way to feelings.
Miles of sand beckon us to keep moving,
demanding we take off our sandals
and wade up to our knees in the crashing waves.
Laughter and smiles break the cares of yesterday
urging us to cuddle close, wade deeper,
          and splash through the surf.

Back to Ship's Point

Four days of bliss faded as we rode the highway
back to our old life, back to the mindless routines,
      to a world that does not care.
Routines evolved into stress, stress into anxiety.
      Old patterns emerged again.
Unkind thoughts led to unkind words.
A new depth of sadness descended.
We lost what had been so precious.

Yet, a new determination materialized
to recapture those moments that were lost,
that hug and a kiss beyond the shores of time,
the love we shared as we walked the endless beach,
the joy of running through the waves,
the blissful peace of drifting with the tides.

Shades of Sadness
from the Future

Precious Hours

The sadness of seeing my son and his family leave after a week-long visit knowing it will be a long time before I see them again.

Dreams come true for a while
 and then they are gone,
disappearing along the highway
that takes them away for me.
As I relive these warm feelings after they depart,
I tuck them safely away in my treasure chest.
I find a place to store them close to my heart.
I quietly relive the precious memories,
the precious hours below the host of stars
where we chatted going deeply into the dark night.

These memories will inevitably sail silently away
leaving just a soft touch of sadness in their wake,
so I diligently translate these feelings into words,
searching for the right lines to harbor them forever.

In the cold days ahead when dark clouds hide the sun
I will retrace these words into these feelings
until I understand why the years pass so swiftly by,
why life has to be filled with ecstasy and sadness,
                 why the father-son bond
                 makes the sadness worthwhile.

The Future Has Arrived

The sadness of arriving at the future, seeing how things turned out, but not being able to tell your past self.

(Koenig p.ix)

The future has arrived.
I am seventy-five,
an age I used to think was very old.
I finally have all the answers.
I know how things turn out in the end.
But they are so different than the life I had planned.

My friends have all disappeared.
I have lost the people I took for granted.
My choices have led me to trials and tribulations.
They have forced me to finally understand the truth,
a wisdom I want to share with my other selves,
the child doing the best he could
         under impossible circumstances,
the young man who started out on his journey
         with hopes and dreams.

There is a small part of me that wants to stay behind,
to relive the past in thoughts and feelings,
to warn my other selves of the pitfalls that lay ahead.
But I am frozen in a hard cold reality
         unable to pass on the truth
         that could have saved them.
I can not go back in time to warn them
that the days are so short and the nights are so long,
athe journey is more important than the destination.

I cannot encourage them to believe in themselves,
to hold on to their dreams and sail with them
into the horizon even when the seas are rough
and the shore seems unreachable.
I would urge them to take time to enjoy
the thrill that doing the impossible brings.
We would face the wildness of the surging seas
                    and laugh.

But my friends did not make it to the end.
They have died along the way.
They are not here to celebrate with me
the joy of finally being able to love ourselves,
and realize dreams are not supposed to come true,
they are just a passage to the great calm blue sea.

            But we would discover
            that the future has turned out
            exactly how it was supposed to be.

The Traveler

*The sadness of the awareness of how little of the world
we'll experience.*

Am I wasting time travelling around the world?
Should I be doing something useful with my life?
Am I a just traveler in search of a dream
that is someone else's reality?
Why do I spend time on planning things
that seem more interesting than the present?
Am I wasting time seeking countless experiences
just to prove I have enough wealth to be alive?

I have lived two years or more on three continents
and in five provinces of my own beloved Canada,
my home, where I live and have my being.
But it is just a small part of the world,
a small part of an even bigger universe
filled with the wonders of the unknown.
There is still a desire to explore more unseen worlds,
to escape the confinement of walls and time,
for the chance to see beyond the horizons.

Now that I have the freedom of time and money
I can set my imagination free to reactivate fantasies.
I can crave to be a citizen of a greater community.
I can conjure up a vision of where I wish to go,
            of whom I wish to be.

The Homebody

I still have this fear of missing out on something
that is right here under my very nose,
an emotion connected of this piece of the world
      that I love so dearly
where I can quietly grasp wisdom from books
by people who have more knowledge than me,
where I occupy the background and the foreground,
transcend fear that I am a lesser version of myself
and seek to engage all my senses, with a calm mind
      and with an open heart.
I have the motivation to keep living and discovering,
to engage in my own private search
      for that private understanding
      that the journey into my soul
is the ultimate adventure of all adventures,
      the ultimate carpe diem.

Imagery from a Poet

The sadness of realizing that that the best we may
be able to do will never be good enough.

Let's not talk of imaginary roses,
or the gray sky of sorrow,
or the will and patience
to wait for a new tomorrow.
Let's be raw like a steak,
callous like an old farmer's hand,
evil as a mosquito sucking blood.

No, even more,
let's be weird like a jigsaw puzzle
with twenty missing pieces,
or gentle like number 20 sandpaper.
Let's quit the similes
and just go straight for the metaphors,
an old man without teeth
whose words have lost their bite,
a discouraged poet
whose last words are wandering
 in the digital wilderness.

The Last Memory

We had a friend over yesterday. He looked thin and tattered having lived a hard life and now facing a serious medical problem. Our conversation turned to the topic of dying with dignity. He said, "We should all have that magic pink pill so we can go out with a celebration, one last good memory for those we love."

There is just one word left to say,
just one more thought to think,
just one more moment to live,
just one more set of lips to kiss,
just one more sigh to sigh,
before I turn my face to the wind,
tuck myself in and say goodbye.

I am no longer angry with the world.
I no longer wish to mold it
to my own version of what it should be.
I am no longer angry with life
for deceiving me and shaping me,
into a man who cannot control
the functions of my own brain.

I am at peace with the world.
I am at peace with life.
I am at peace with me.
I am at peace with death.
I am ready to kiss my love good-bye.
I am ready to say 'ready' and die.

Shades of Sadness
from Being a Poet

Ode to the Poet

The anxiety of not knowing the real me. (Oh, by the way, the chaotic rhyme patterns are on purpose.)
(Koenig p. 68).)

I digest other people's emotions.
Like a dog I vomit them
and swallow them back up again
so I can regurgitate the me,
the me I want others to see,
so I can survive with the real me intact.

I have contradictory moods and urges
that can control me at any given time.
It is hard for me to say
who I am going to be today.
I am a like a social mirror
reflecting whichever image comes near.

I play different roles at different times.
I can employ modern psychology
pretending to understand the rhymes
of the human minds exposed so humbly,
while I struggle to understand my own.

I can be an intellect with profound thoughts
garnered from achieving three degrees,
supported by a lifetime of searching through plots,
striving to share my brilliant theories
with anyone who will listen.

I can be a respected mystic
melding the science of psychology
with knowledge gained by sharing my essence
with the universal presence,
delving into the mysteries of the human identity,
creating an imaginary bridge to an altered reality.

If I could only restore myself
to the innocence I was seventy-six years ago,
I would wipe out the me others wanted me to be.
I would tearfully peal the bitter onion.
and strip down my self-image function by function.

I would reshape my habits,
eliminate things that distract me...
the restraints imposed by my family,
the false concepts of my education,
my programming, my cultural indoctrination.

Then I could finally reveal the real me
not just the me I want everyone to see.
Perhaps I would rediscover myself in art,
my identity in the random brush strokes,
a collection of dancing colors on a white chart.

Perhaps the real me is in these sad poems
a compilation of phrases no one wants to read,
because they do not want to see the pattern,
the repetitions, the rhythm, the rhyme,
the similes and metaphors out of place out of time.

Perhaps this is the real me,
a collection of awkward abstract symbols
scattered across a blank page,
attempts to make a random impression
on a world slipping into silent rage.

The Poet Who Is not a Poet

Perhaps the poet is not the real me.
Perhaps I should eliminate the imagery and rhymes
        and just be me.

Perhaps I am only the me I want to be
when I pour out my broken heart to a friend.
Perhaps I am the real me when I sit quietly,
listen, and respond from the heart,
not as an intellect, or a mystic, or even a poet
        but just as a friend...
        ... just as a friend.

Becoming Invisible

Longing to disappear completely; to melt into a crowd and become invisible, so you can take in the world without having to be part of it.

(Koenig p. 9)

Introvert's Delema

The dilemma of being an introvert haunts me.
I desire to be seen, to be heard, to be invincible,
but to let myself be vulnerable is inconceivable.
so I choose to stay by myself, quietly invisible.

Poet's Delema

They must never hear my poems inner plea.
They must never know my heart's vulnerability,
They must not be allowed to watch and realize
 I am not the cautious person I pretend to be.

Poet's Advantage

The advantage of being a poet saves me.
I search for a sidewalk café, alone.
My eyes dart here and there,
looking for an empty table with an empty chair.

I hide in observation and contemplation.
I avoid manipulation and conversation.
I hide my human eyes with dark glasses
waiting until the anxious moment passes.

I reflect just what I want others to see.
I take out my notepad and set my words free.
I let my imagination see what it wants to see.
I cloak raw emotions in sad shades of mystery.

I pass my emotions on to others raw to the bone,
           but not my bones.
I have no spoken words I want to share.
I save it all for lines of print few will ever read.
I smile and try to tell myself I don't really care.

Imperfect Poems

Wanting to share something special with a friend only to be saddened as you see all the work's flaws for the first time.

(Koenig p.14)

My poetry is personal to me.
I write to express my thoughts
so I can see them on paper
so I can ponder their significance
      to me,
        just to me.

But sometimes my cautious mind is not careful.
My words take on a meaning from my soul.
My heart seizes the opportunity to share itself.
I print out the words and hold my breath.
      I share my poems.
I search the faces for signs of compassion.

As I wait the words come back to haunt me.
      I see every flaw,
every awkward word and phrase,
every comma that is out of place.
I wish I had gone over it one more time
      and perfected every line
before I placed my mind on my heart's altar.

And then the smile that says they understand
appears in their eyes and flows down to their lips.
They say, 'I think I know you better now,
      I think I love you more.'

Guilty

The sadness of feeling shame instead of pride when you have done something good.

(Koenig p. 52)

It went beautifully,
my recital as poet laureate
to the inauguration of the new city council.
It was that treasured moment of connection
between the poet and those who listen and hear
the sad heartbeat of humanity.

I made a statement for the homeless,
for those lost in their own minds,
for my indigenous sisters and brothers
trying to fit into a world that doesn't care,
for all those unable to catch their breath
in a fast-paced indifferent Canadian society.

I could feel it, that energy,
that beautiful energy.
They were with me all the way.
People greeted me warmly.
The mayor sought me out to thank me.

Then it hit me ...that old familiar feeling...
... guilt...
... shame...
...more than shame...
... dread.
I had exposed my private thoughts in public.
I had let them see my heart and soul.

I packed up and left as fast as I could.
I sat in my car in the parking lot...
  --- shaking...
   ... unable to breathe.
I reached into my soul.
I held onto the spirit of self-love,
until my lungs could fill with air again.

Innocent

I am innocent. I did nothing wrong.
The prosecutor had no right to detain me,
no right to accuse me of breaking the law of silence.
There should be no remorse, no regrets.

But it is what it is.
I have to love the prosecutor
for doing what prosecutors do,
punishing the guilty and protecting the innocent.
But I am more than innocent.
I am part of the greater good.
  I am a poet.
Most of us are the shy sort,
only comfortable alone
in a quiet place with pen in hand.
  But I do what poets do.
We shout out against injustice.
We dare to draw attention to ourselves
so others can see what we see
and feel what we feel.
We sacrifice ourselves on the alter of compassion.
We let our voices quiver.
We sometimes cry.
We cry so others can cry.

But

But……
if I could only….
        … if only…
        … I could…
              … be proud…
              … of what I do…
              … and who I am.

Too Near the Sun

A crisis of self doubt

(Koenig p. 55)

I have flown too near the hot sun.
I can feel the wax
that holds my wings together
melt in the cold-heat of indifference.
I am falling.
I am losing my desire to be,
my desire to write.

I love to write poems.
I spend the early morning hours
getting in touch with the spirit in me
who touches my soul
until my soul touches my mind
with warm thoughts,
and my fingers begin to fly
oblivious of the world around me.

Each book of poetry is a thousand hours
of feeling feelings too hot to bear
feelings that demand the presence of tears
to quench the burning inside.
So I continue to write my deepest feelings
knowing no one listens, no else cares.

I am surrounded by boxes of books
that refuse to sell themselves.
But what else can I do
to fill these aging hours,
to express these intense thoughts,

to feel these desperate feelings,
given only to me
to be shared with anyone who will listen.
And so I fly as near to the sun as I can fly
lugging my books to bookstores
seeking the warmth of a smile
avoiding indifference that can melt wings.

I realize I may never fly near the sun again.
I no longer want to think.
I no longer want to feel.
I do not want to see sad movies
I do not want to write sad poems.

Yet I am one of a million poets
struggling to be heard
by our fellow human beings
knowing that perhaps a few
will see what we see
and feel what we feel.

So I have come back to Earth.
I have landed on my feet.
I attend book fairs
just for the opportunity
to give my books away
to the precious few who may care.

Nothing New

The sadness that occurs when we realize that originality is no longer possible.

Koneg p. 8

Solomon got it right,
There's nothing new under the sun.
Trying to be unique is an exercise in futility.
Even my poems, the creations of my soul,
    are not unique.

I long to be different, to stand out from the crowd,
              but what a crowd it is,
over eight billion people on this planet,
and a hundred million poets trying to be unique,
saying the same thing in a billion different ways.

As a poet, I recognize my search for recognition
            is slowly killing me.
It adds a another 'why bother' to my box of excuses.
Hopelessness turns my poems into something sad,
something that can never reach the level of happy,
a collection of images that are almost identical
to an unending litany of sad poems
written in a hundred different languages
by poets just like me with the same sad feelings
expressed in a hundred million different ways.

Unique but the Same

I step away from my self-created shades of sadness.
I take comfort I am part of the brotherhood of poets.
Each one of us lives and writes in our dark closet
        unique... but the same.
We spend the late-night hours writing bleak poems
written is a passion that speaks separate truths
        unique... but the same.
Each poem is written in a specific time and place
by the workings of a mind celebrating its aloneness
        unique ...but the same.
We share ourselves so this world can find a safe place
where people can endure all the shades of sadness
        and I learn to cry.

Made in the USA
Las Vegas, NV
16 December 2023

82292816R00052